GROWING PAINS

Written By

JaShunna Boykins

ISBN-9798853022195

Library of Congress Control Number: 2018675309
Printed in the United States of America

I dedicate this book to every little black girl and every black woman who has ever struggled to find her voice in the midst of chaos. I hear you. I see you. I feel you. I am you.

CONTENTS

"Cry your heart out
clean you face
when you're in doubt
go at your own pace."
-Adele

MY CUP SPILLETH OVER

This space that I'm in is dark and unfamiiar, territory that I've never treaded upon. This fog has clouded my mind and I can't see, but I've grown weak and weary. So, being blind will just have to do. You see, at one point in time my cup runneth over, but somewhere along the way my hope, faith, and desire to live spilled out, so this emptiness is all I'm left with. I woke up this morning with every intention to tackle my to-do list, but lying down in this twin size bed tucked away in my college dorm is all I've got. While I'm on this zoom call, I should probably be following along and taking notes,

but lying here until my name is called for attendance is all I've got. My friends want to go to the cafe to grab something to eat, but I really don't have it in me to leave this room, so I just won't eat today because what's missing a few meals when I'd rather not be here anyway?

I know my mama will call and want to hear about my day. I

don't have the strength to tell her how I really feel, neither do I

have the luxury of missing her phone call so instead,

I'll just pretend to be busy and rush her off the phone because

just letting her hear the sound of my voice is all I've got.

I want to go out and socialize but watching tv alone in my room

is all I've got. I really like this new guy but my own problems

are in the way so being friends with him is all I've got.

I should get up and get dressed and attempt to tackle

the day but crying in the shower is all I've got.

I want to live a life of peace and prosperity, but

depression and despair is all I've got...

left in this cup that spilleth over.

IT'S NOT WHAT IT LOOKS LIKE

I really don't want to get out of my bed because I'm so comfortable and I just feel like being "lazy" today. At least that's what I'll tell my friends. I haven't had an appetite lately but I'll just say it's because I don't like eating the food on campus; this way no one asks any more questions. I haven't been to my in-person classes, but I'll just say that they were canceled or better yet moved to zoom so no one is concerned. I really don't want any company, but I guess I'll entertain for a few hours to laugh and share tik-toks so it won't appear that I'm "acting funny". Here I am painting a different picture for those who care for me, so that they won't see me through my lens. In reality, I couldn't get out of this bed even if I wanted to. I can't eat. I barely sleep. And no, I'm not acting funny, but I'd rather you not know how far gone I really am.

SO ANXIOUS

Thoughts swirling

Palms sweating

Heart racing

Hands trembling

Panic surfacing

People staring

Some laughing

They say I'm faking

But if only they knew…

I wish I was.
Tears falling

Breath shaking

Feet pacing

Body aching

Spirit breaking

Soul crying
It feels like I'm dying
But if only they
knew… I wish I was.

ANTI-DEPRESSANT

I came to you for help
against my better judgment
Standing on my last leg, I used you for leverage
resting all my weight on you.
You were supposed to give me my life back, help me take
a load off Cause' there was so much I had to unpack.
Darkness was consuming everything around me.
I was fumbling around in the dark. Damn, can I get some light
around here? I was looking for you to be the spark...
A lamp if you will, so maybe I can find my will to live again
cause' all I ever think about these days is dying.
I'm hoping peace will be on the other side, a place where there's no more
crying. I needed you to get me there fast cause I'm tired of trying.
I came to you for help because I didn't want to
do anything irrational. I'm letting you take the
wheel so I won't act on how I feel.
But that wasn't the best decision.
Because in the blink of an eye you decided to abort your mission. In a
matter of time something shifted in me all because I let you take the lead.
Now I'm looking for different ways to leave this place because you've
convinced me that I'll never find what I'm looking for in this space.
Instead of using your powers for good, you festered my mind
with darker thoughts and drove me over the deep end.
I came to you for help, against my better judgment
Because I considered you to be a friend.

SEPTEMBER 24, 2021- DAY 1

I'd much rather be back on campus watching movies and looking at funny tik-toks but it feels good not to stress about school for a few days. Since I've been here my stress levels have gone down. My thoughts are becoming more positive and my mind is no longer racing. My headache went away with no medication. My family and friends have reassured me that I don't need to rush to reach a certain level of success. I'm only 20, I've got nothing but time to get myself together but I must first learn to be patient with myself. I don't actually want to die, I just need to find an effective way to cope with my present situation. I need to remember that God operates outside of time, so things will fall into place when they're supposed to.

SEPTEMBER 25, 2021- DAY 2

Last night I had a little trouble falling asleep because I'm in an unfamiliar place. But nonetheless, I still got plenty of rest. After chatting with others within the group I have a new perspective. As of now I no longer wish to harm myself. If anything, I'm excited about facing my reality outside these doors and pacing myself to reach my goals. There's no right or wrong way to get my degree and whenever I do, I'll be one step closer to helping my community. When I heard the relief in my families' voices after knowing I was safe, I was so proud of myself for getting the help I needed and deciding not to carry out my plan of ending my life. I now realize that I don't give myself the same amount of grace that I extend to others. Once I learn to do so, the suicidal thoughts will become easier to combat.

BITTERSWEET ESCAPE

I'd never thought I'd get here,

Coming to you out of all people for relief.

But at this point in time, I've got nothing to lose.

You've never been my cup of tea but it's safe

to say my taste buds have evolved.

The truth is, I'm desperate so what could it hurt to

give you a try. Breaking down my inner most deepest

thoughts, just to stuff, tuck, and roll them away.

Bringing you to my lips, with a flick of the lighter,

I spark a flame to your bosom.

Deep breath in, I inhale your goodness

Within a matter of seconds I exhale my pain.

I repeat the process until I'm no longer touching earth. I've

elevated. I sit with the clouds in a whole 'nother state of mind.

I feel weightless and full of bliss.

But I find this to be short lived.

As my high comes down, plummeting back down

to earth, anxiety creps back in, intrusive thoughts begin to

resurface and I realize that I'm now back to my

painful–what seems to be– inescapable reality. But

in the end I guess it was worth a shot.

Such a bittersweet escape.

POKER FACE

You look at me and wonder why I seem to be in deep thought. Little do you know, I'm talking myself off the ledge for the umpteenth time today. You look at me and see just another resting bitch face. Little do you know, on the inside, I'm wasting away.

NOT YOUR NEGRO SPIRITUAL

When you go to lay down your burdens by the
riverside, Do you ever wish you could take me?
I must be your heaviest load considering
the weight of all the baggage I carry.

MAMA NEVER SAID THERE'D BE DAYS LIKE THIS

What do you do when you're tired but can't seem to find rest?

What do you do when you have nothing left to give
but yet you're still trying your best?

Where do you go to find sanctuary when everything in
your life causes strife but offers no peace?

What do you do when your body is weary and you can't find relief?

What do you do when it seems like you have more reasons to die than to live?

What do you do when you've given all you've got,
and there's nothing left to give?

NOT YOUR SUPERWOMAN

The rest of the would rather stand back & applaud Black Women for our strength than to straighten up their acts in order to lighten the load they forced us to carry. Our shoulders aren't your resting place, if we can't count on your arms for a soft embrace.

Our backs weren't made to be saddled,

to ride you all into your own justices—

for ourselves to be left with nothing.

WISHFUL THINKING

As a Black woman,

there's nothing more I'd rather be than,

SEEN.

HEARD.

FELT.

HELD..

PROTECTED.

CARESSED.

CHERISHED.

LOVED.

FREE.

As a Black woman, there's nothing more I'd
rather be, than ME, unapologetically.

DEAR BLACKNESS,

All my life, society has taught me to hate you, be ashamed of you, be anything but proud to have you as a part of me. For a long time, I second guessed my worth because you were a factor. But it's not you that causes hurt and pain, it's the distorted image the rest of the world paints of you-the mere hatred of you. Being told that there's only one way to be black and the tormenting stereotypes that come along with it have left me questioning myself many a night. Existing in the world as a dark skin black woman does nothing but add on to the hatred spewed against my flesh. But nonetheless, it wasn't until I became an adult, that I grew to appreciate Blackness, in all your glory, power, and essence. It's an honor and privilege to embrace you and become one with you. You are the blueprint for everything that is beautiful.
Sincerely,

A Beautiful Black Woman.

BLACKITY BLACK-BLACK

My black is beautiful.

My black don't crack.

My black is a blessing.

My black is rich in melanin.

Yes, my black is dark.

My black is sweet.

My black possesses a power that can't be
beat. My black is angelic, never apologetic.

My black will never accept defeat.
My black is never lacking.

So stand back and watch me
adjust my crown, cause' my black
makes the world go round.'

SAY MY NAME

To all my black girls around the world,

Make them say your name.

There is BEAUTY in your name.

There is POWER in your name.

Your identity starts and ends with your name.

How dare you condense yourself for the convenience
of another? Your name is never a bother.
Make them SAY YOUR NAME!

DEAR AMERICA,

So what if I am the angry black woman?

I have every right to be.

You've given me and my foremothers nothing but heartache and pain since our feet touched the soil. Your continued acts of hatred towards me make my blood boil. Does my attitude offend you? You think I do too much?

Well you have none other but yourself to blame,

And you ain't seen nothing yet.

I am angry.

I'm pissed off.

I'm mad as hell.

You've shitted on the black woman for long enough, so it's about time I raise hell.

IT IS WHAT IT IS

"Well you know it is what it is."

Said every black person who felt as if their feelings weren't valid.
Said every black person who seemed to have exhausted their
resources. A declaration of defeat is what that was.
" Hey, it is what it is."

Said every black person that has given up hope.

You said our pain didn't matter so that's how
we cope. A declaration of defeat is
what that was.
This country has taken away so much and yet

we still haven't been allotted the proper time to heal.

For our time to recover is now.

Your reign of terror is coming to an end.

So, it is what it is.

A declaration of war, is what that was.

DEAR MAMA,

If diamonds are a girl's best friend,

then you're the most precious jewel.

Your value is immeasurable.

I could give you the world and everything in it and still be in
debt unto you. Your love for me is God- like–unconditional.
Like you are none other; you're irreplaceable.

Dear sweet mother, oh how I wish you could
live forever. I'd choose you in any lifetime–
whenever, wherever, whatever.

LOVE LETTER TO MUSIC

You have the ability to read my mind

You finish my sentences

You fill in the blanks with words I can never seem to find. You send chills
down my spine. You possess a beauty that simply cannot be defined.
Each note expresses every emotion I've ever
experienced. You are truly an extension of God.
Your possibilities are endless.

A timeless masterpiece that goes on forever–

Infinite.

IT'S NOT ME YOU LOVE

I know that I'm not here because you wanted me, but because you
craved her in that moment which turned into the birthing of a
new life. As the years pass and this adolescent grows it becomes
very clear to me– I mean everybody knows that in the
midnight hour when you decide to show your face, in this
space, to grace me with your presence, that my face
wasn't the one that you were missing.

When I got my own means of communication, your voice was the
one I looked forward to hearing. Yet, it was always her phone that was
ringing. Yeah 'cause see mama ain't raise no fool... but I guess because
you empty your wallet a few times for me we're supposed to be cool.
'Nah you see that's the funny part, your money doesn't move
me. It was your heart and your time and affection that I wanted
from the start. But it seems to me that I'm asking for too much
or is it the wrong mouth from which these words depart?
I get it. You still love her, & I understand why.

She's a beautiful woman and I get to call her my mother.
Is it fair for me to be envious and resentful at times when
the pain I feel is being inflicted by another?
Deep down I know that you'll never love me as much
as you love her and it hurts like hell.
And now I've got some healing to do but only time will tell

when that day will come.

But it hurts even more to know that so many have felt this
same pain so they know where I'm coming from.
See all we wanted was to be daddy's little girl, but I guess
some dreams are too far fetched for this world.

THE BLAME GAME

Was it something I did?

Or maybe something I said,

Can someone please explain?

What'd I do to be deserving of such pain?

I didn't ask for all those lies you fed.

Why am I not good enough?

I share your blood and she even gave me your last name. You set back and let me take the blame for your shortcomings yet, you feel no shame.

Is it really me at fault?

In all my attempts I failed to make you love me. But maybe it's because it was never my place to earn it but for you to freely give it.

FOREIGN LANGUAGE

You look me in my eyes and tell me

sweet little lies.

They leave such a bitter taste behind.

Lucky for me, my taste buds have adapted.

You look me in my eyes and tell me unwarranted lies.

That must be your love language.

Lucky for me , your words are foreign because the only language I can speak as well as understand is the truth. Too bad for you it's not in your vocabulary.

So if the question is do you really love me?

I guess we'll never know.

You've uttered those words a thousand times but your actions never show. You look me in my eyes and tell me beautiful lies. You said you love me and think the world of me....

Say it ain't so.

BEHIND CLOSED DOORS

Little black girls getting touched by their family members
must be some sort of rite of passage.
Our bodies are never really our own.

Any and everything we do gets labeled as "grown".

Just cause' we develop wide hips and thick thighs,

Doesn't give you permission to have harassing hands or
wondering eyes. But we dare not speak up to seek justice.
Because, well you know how the phrase goes,

What happens in this house, stays in this house.

STICKS AND STONES

The power of life and death are in the tongue,

So it seems to me that you've chosen violence.

You knew your words were killing me.

However, I love you too much to ever do you the
same so for your sake, I choose silence.
I suggest you expand your vocabulary before you
end up with my blood on your hands.

CALLING YOU OUT

Why is it that people feel as if they've cured your
depression when they tell you to just pray?
Even God said faith without works is dead.

The truth is, you spoke out of ignorance to fill a
void Because you knew of nothing else to say.
But His word will never return unto
Him void. So thanks, but no thanks.
I'll take His advice instead.

ALONE BUT NOT LONELY

I'd like to think that I'm a loner because

I prefer my own company over that of others.

Some would call me an introvert.

I stay to myself.

But the reality is, I'd rather ghost you than let you get rid of me. To avoid strife , I just choose to be alone,
rather to be left alone when you decide to leave from by my side and walk out of my life.

LAUGH TO KEEP FROM CRYING

While laughter is good for the
soul, In my chest, there's a hole.
It's filled with anger and
depression & with each trial,
there's a lesson If I learn
to get over my past,
Then maybe my joy will finally last.

NOVEMBER 13, 2021

I think I found the root of my depression. I feel like an extra, maybe I'm not essential. Which would explain why I spent a lot of my time trying to be a part of every extracurricular activity. Trying to find my place. I feel as if I were to eliminate myself, nothing would change, no one would be affected by my not being here. Or maybe they'll be better off because I won't be a waste of space. I feel as if I have to accomplish something grand and when I fall short, I feel like the biggest failure in the world, no longer worthy of life.

NOVEMBER 29, 2021

I feel like I've reached a point where I no longer care. I don't care if things get better or worse for me. I don't care if they stay the same. I don't care to try anymore. I don't care whether I live or die. I'm tired of trying to make things better so I don't care to fight this depression anymore. I'm tired of praying the same prayers, crying the same tears, tired of venting, tired of hoping–just tired. I feel as if I've accepted that this is all life has to offer me. No matter how many times I find the strength to get back up, I end up further down in darkness than before. It's like my eyes have adjusted to being in a dark room. I know I can't see, but I've grown comfortable.

DECEMBER 2, 2021

Another day of pressing on but at the same time feeling hopeless. As the days have passed, each night when I go to sleep, I think to myself that I wouldn't be mad if I didn't wake up. I'm to the point that the only thing keeping me here is the unknown.

Not knowing if my mama can handle living without me, or not knowing if I'm right on the edge of a breakthrough but I miss it because I gave up too early.

This place of uncertainty hurts. It hurts to cry, to take a deep breath, to think that even with all of this fighting, I'm not fighting hard enough. It hurts– to be low on strength, low on faith, low on hope, low on time. I don't want to let this darkness consume me, but it hurts to fight it. I've been in the same storm for so long that I've stopped looking for the sun.

JUST ANOTHER CHORE

Taking out the trash can feel like such a dirty
task. Things can get messy in the process.
Getting rid of all things disposable,

anything that no longer holds value.

Everything that no longer serves a
purpose must go. Anything.
Everything.

Even if that thing...

is me.

OFF THE DEEP END

I constantly find myself at a tug of war with my mind over
my will to live, And I'm slowly losing my grip.
I'm tipping on the tightrope,

One wrong step and I might slip.

Falling to my demise.

THE CLOCK IS TICKING

You told me to hold on just a little while longer, But
this is a matter of life or death so even that is too long.

DECEMBER 3, 2021

Yesterday, I got a word from God. While it wasn't what I wanted to hear, it was the very thing I needed. I understand that this storm is my preparation considering how I want to be able to counsel others, & I can't truly empathize and help people if I've never been down and out myself. I know that things won't get easier. However, I'll be better equipped to handle my problems. Instead of focusing on my goals in their entirety, I should focus on laying one brick at a time. It's still dark where I am right now but I'm starting to see the light at the end of the tunnel.

MASTER OF DISGUISE

Depression is not a "one-size-fits-all" kind of girl.

She comes in all different shapes and sizes.

Depression wears many faces.

She can show up serving you glitz and glam,

Or you could catch her carrying heavy eye bags while
flashing a broken smile. She's just that versatile.
Depression can shape shift to fill even the smallest spaces.

Her feet are as light as a burglar creeping through your house at
night. She's manipulative and conniving; she doesn't mind getting
her hands dirty. Depression will make you do things against your
own will. She gives a whole new meaning to peer pressure.
She made me give her piggy back rides just so she could weigh me
down. She forced herself upon me and our bodies were intertwined.
My mind became hers and her thoughts became mine.
She tied an anchor to my ankle and tossed me in
the sea in hopes that I might drown.
Depression wanted to take my life as a trophy to add to her display
case. She took me through hell and back, but I left her there.
Depression is one hell of a fighter, but it's safe to say I'm one hell of a survivor.

GROWING PAINS

I'm venturing out on a new journey. But not just any journey, this one
is focused on healing. The state of being that I'm currently in no longer
serves me. I must address the pain that I've been suppressing for so long. I
can't lie, this process is tedious, it's uncomfortable, it's painful, but it's also
necessary. Nonetheless, new opportunities, new beginnings, new grace, new
mercies are awaiting me on the other side. Having a sense of self awareness
pushes me to want to reach my fullest potential, and I know I can't get there
broken. The only option I have is to pick up the pieces, complete the puzzle
and move forward. I thank God for the revelations I've received in order
for me to reach this point in my journey, and for ordering my steps the rest
of the way. I may be going through a storm but I'm excited to see myself
on the other side of it, because flowers can't grow without a little rain.

THE LITTLE THINGS

Skin prepped

Body cleansed

Lights turned low

Favorite candle lit

Blunt rolled

Bed freshly made

Chill playlists on repeat

Blissful mood is set

Happiness has entered the chat

With these simple pleasures, my self care day is complete.

NOTE TO SELF:

No matter how big or small your puzzle piece is,
without it, the puzzle isn't solved.

Without your laugh, the joke is never quite as funny.

Without your 8- count, the routine is never quite finished.

Without your verse, the lyrics are never quite complete.

Without your voice, the harmony is never quite blended.

Without your period, a sentence has never quite ended

Act like you know who you are.

Worthy indeed, disposable you are not.

You've been casted for this role, now play your part.

BLURRED VISION

I wish you could see what God sees

Beautifully and wonderfully made

God broke the mold

You're one of one

With a heart of gold

You exude light

Your melanin glows

You're simply the shit & everybody knows…
Everyone except you.
I wish you could see what God sees.

Beautifully and wonderfully made with a
purpose. One of God's greatest creations.
A gift to mankind.

Called.

Chosen.

Destined to do great things.

You were made whole.

Nothing missing.
Nothing broken.

Enough. Just as you are.

Why can't you see what God sees?

GIRL, GIVE YOURSELF SOME GRACE

You chase after perfection, as if you could ever catch it.

Moving towards and unreachable mark

and like so many times before

you're face to face with defeat .

Once again , your self-worth depletes .

Only because you've measured yourself up against a criteria you could never meet. So do yourself a favor,

Strive to be better at least it's an attainable feat.

ARE YOU IN GOOD HANDS?

Whether or not you suffer by your own hand Or
the hands of another, if you take your struggles
to God, you'll always be in good hands.

DEAR YOUNGER SELF,

I'm sorry for lying to you.

I allowed the actions of others convince you that

you had to do something in order to be someone.

Your self-worth should never be equated to any
accomplishment or the lack thereof.
Because the truth of the matter is,

Your very existence means you're enough.

GOT TO GIVE IT UP

Learn to forgive.

Before you give all your time and energy to a situation
you cannot change. Learn to forgive,
before you give up your beauty rest in exchange
for sleepless nights. Learn to forgive,
before you give your enemies power to change your
whole demeanor at the mere sight of them.
Learn to forgive.

For holding a grudge does nothing but form fine lines across
your face that only the process of letting go can erase.
I know you may think that this is the way to ensure they'll
never get away with the pain they made you endure.
But please take heed to my words

Learn to forgive.

Before you waste away all your years on bitterness ,
hatred and angry tears. You've got to forgive,
For you have got more life to live.

ME V. ME

I went to war within myself for the me that I wanted
to be; my mind was the battlefield.
I clothed myself with the full armor of God and

I hid God's word within my heart as a secret weapon against
my enemies. I ventured on a quest to find them .
Abandonment. Anger. Anxiety. Bitterness. Depression.
Unforgiveness, I called them out by their names,
conquering them one by one. I vowed to never
stop fighting, until my victory was won.

MIRROR MIRROR ON THE WALL

I find myself looking at my reflection in the mirror,

but this image isn't familiar.

Of Course we share the same face,

She has the same piercing eyes,

Afrocentric nose, and small yet full lips.

She's got my round behind and curved out hips.

It's not her body that I fail to recognize.

It's her thoughts, the sound of her voice, the cadence in which she walks, with such grace and poise. I asked God to do a work within me and He laid the old me to rest. The woman who is now looking back at me is perhaps His best work yet.

IN THE LAND OF THE LIVING

I am yet alive because I serve a living
God. God who calls me by my name.
God who stays the same.

God who holds me tight when I lie awake at
night. God who lets me know everything's gonna
be alright. I live because God lives in me.

THINKING OUT LOUD

Could it be that our life stories are meant to reflect
who and what God is according to
Who and what we allow God to be in our lives?

PERCEPTION IS EVERYTHING

To some, we'll always be the villain in their story
because we've only ever shown them our flaws.
To others, we'll always be good in their eyes
because they choose to see past our scars.
The truth is, no one is all good.

Nor are they all bad.

But that's what makes life beautiful.

Nothing is ever just black or white.

ANXIOUS EYES

Anxious eyes, desperate for help, stare back at me.

Pleading for help in exchange of the words she
cannot speak. How can I help, what can I do?
I must get this girl to gather the strength to pull through.

Breathe in, breathe out. Focus your eyes on me.

Our souls connected, only speaking through energy.

Unhelpful spirits gather around, distracting her focus with their
negative sounds. Ignore them, I got you. Look only at me.
Keep on with those deep breaths. I promise you're safe
with me. Minutes feel like days as her heart rate slows.
Breathing returns to normal and her ability to speak grows.

We made it through another one, this one easier than the
last. My prayer is that one day this is all a part of her past.
She is ok but tired, so resilient, strong and brave. Anxiety will not
consume her, cause I will be there by her side every step of the way.
Written By Kristal Poland

IN THE SHADOWS

In shadows cast by weary minds, I
stand as a guide when hope unwinds.
A counselor's path, a solemn role, To
aid a heart in depths unknown. Within
these walls, where silence speaks,
Depression's weight, its anguish leaks.
A fragile soul with fears entwined,
Seeking solace, a light to find.
Anxiety, a restless dance,

Like whispers, racing thoughts
advance. In trembling steps,
we'll navigate, Through anxious
storms, we'll liberate. And in
the darkest of despair,
Suicidal whispers fill the air.

But I'll be there, a
steadfast guide, To quell
the tides of suicide.
With empathy, a gentle art,

I'll hold your hand, mend every part.
Together, we'll unearth the dawn,
And forge a path where hope is
drawn. In words unspoken, tears
released, A healing journey, pain
decreased. With every step, we'll find
our way, To brighter skies, a brand-
new day. For as a counselor, I see,
The strength that lies deep within
thee. And though the road may twist
and bend, Together, we'll find strength
to mend. So trust in me, your burdens
share, For in this space, I deeply care.

With an open heart and listening ear,
We'll face the darkness, without fear.

Written by Kasey Myers

A BEAUTIFUL SOUL

A beautiful soul deserves a beautiful life.
How could they not see her?
Why would they not believe her cries?
She was yelling, screaming to be seen and heard.
She was brave, bold, and daring.
I've never met a soul like hers and at such a tender age with the talents of the world, carrying the burdens of her ancestors, fighting for every breath.
Supporting this soul was a duty and honor, I didn't take it lightly.
She was our purpose, the reason why we were called here.
We could not let her give up.
She's a fighter, that's for sure. So courageous and strong.
And we were her protectors.
We stood firm and true.
To witness the pain of this beautiful soul felt like torture.
I knew better than to question it, but I wanted to take it away.
We did everything we could so she could shine bright and be free.
Together, this beautiful soul found her way out of the darkness and into the light. Now, she radiates so vividly.
I wonder if this beautiful soul knows how much she's given me.

Written by Jenesis Gibson

AS YOUR COUSIN

When you were sad and depressed I was there to calm the stress.
While you were sad and down I stuck by your side so you wouldn't
drown. There were times you wanted to let go but through
me God said no. Many laughed and didn't understand.
Neither did I.

But I knew whatever it was wouldn't stand a chance.

Now you've tamed and overcame.

You fought till depression was no longer tied

to your name. *Written by NyKeisse Wing*o

THIS TOO SHALL PASS

Looking at the pain in the eyes of someone you love
dearly, Watching with confusion as you're in despair.
Holding out my hand saying trust me, I've got you.

But in reality, you're scared and confused as well.

Even during the darkest times when you felt so alone,

I was right there with you.

Waiting to listen and to try to understand.

All those times I thought you were happy and the
sadness snuck upon you. I was waiting, waiting.
I waited.

I waited and the darkness moved and the sun
began to shine. I'm so glad, so thankful.
I waited.

Written By Aelicia Bledsoe

THE BIGGER PICTURE

It's easy to give up on solving the puzzle, when you don't know
the masterpiece it will be when it's complete...

Just. Keep. Going.

ACKNOWLEDGEMENTS

To my mother, Aelicia, for being my biggest cheerleader.

To my cousin NyKeisse, for his unwavering support.

To my counselors, Ms. Kristal and Ms. Jenesis for going above and beyond in their work.

To my couselor Ms. Kasey who inspired me to take my gift of writing more seriously.

To my high school english teacher Mrs. McConnathy for pouring into me as a student.

To my special friend, Kadrian, who saw the gift of writing in me and pushed me share it with the world.

To all of my family and friends who have supported me thus far.

ABOUT THE AUTHOR

Jashunna Boykins

JaShunna Boykins is a 22 year old black american woman from Logansport,LA. She is currently working towards a degree in psychology from Southern Univerity and A&M College. She has future plans to become a mental health professional and aid in ending the stigma around mental health within the black community. This is her first self-written/self-published book of poetry. In her spare time, she enjoys the simple pleasures, of reading, writing, singing, dancing, and even drawing. She's an all-around creative who enjoys her own company. JaShunna looks forward to writing other projects in the future.

Made in the USA
Columbia, SC
17 June 2024

36805549R00043